Praise for *The A*

"With a tender eloquence that equals the French original, Hélène Cardona brings into English a harrowing tale, *The Abduction* by Maram Al-Masri, of a new mother devastated by the abduction of her son, kidnapped by his father to be raised in Syria. Now, as the distraught mother powerfully notes, "war rages within me." Cardona vividly conveys both palpable love and the wisdom learned from tragic loss: "To love, it is to prepare yourself / to be abandoned." As *The Abduction* proves, Hélène Cardona is a translator who has the exquisite sensitivity and erudition that this brave, vulnerable work deserves."

—Cynthia Hogue,
winner of the Harold Morton Landon
Translation Award from the Academy of American Poets,
author of *In June the Labyrinth*

"Using artfully spare language and repetition, Maram Al-Masri takes us deep into the emotional complexities of losing her young child to a patriarchal society. Hélène Cardona's deft translations capture both the stark immediacy and haunting music of these moving poems, almost letting us believe they were written in English."

—Martha Collins,
author of *Casualty Reports*
and *Because What Else Could I Do*,
winner of the Poetry Society of America's
William Carlos Williams Award

"In maternal bulletins, succinct, austere, and tender, the soul-ravaged speaker of *The Abduction*, like a Syrian Persephone, speaks from the wintry aftermath of her infant son's kidnapping ('dusk no longer has your eyes')—a shocking turn in a contentious divorce battle. The earliest poems in this remarkable sequence convey the female speaker's first euphoric observations of her child and arc to the windfall of her poignant reunion with her son thirteen years later. In the face of this domestic catastrophe, of patriarchal cruelty and callousness, Al-Masri takes a terse, almost elemental approach, employing silence and pared-down lyricism as able tools, reminding us of the poet's champion task ('to write / is to be the boat that saves the drowning') of seeking trusty, precise language for unbearable grief and waiting."

"Each small stanza of *The Abduction* picks at the torn seam between parent and child. As the narrator peers 'out a window/ I haven't cleaned for a long time,' we also see what has been snatched away. Arabic poet Al-Masri writes of the changed shape of her future, a devastation eloquently translated by Hélène Cardona."

The Abduction

Acknowledgements

Gracious thanks to the following literary journals and anthologies where many excerpts first appeared, sometimes in different incarnations:

World Literature Today (Daniel Simon, Ed.)
AGNI (Jennifer Kwon Dobbs, Shuchi Saraswat, Eds.)
On the Sewall (Nancy Naomi Carlson, Translation Ed.; Ron Slate, Ed.)
Plume (Mihaela Moscaliuc, Translation Ed.; Daniel Lawless, Ed.)
Anomaly 25 formerly *Drunken Boat* (Anna Rosenwong, Ed.)
Exchanges: Journal of Literary Translation (Derick Mattern Ed., Iowa
         Translation Staff Eds.)
Agenda Poetry, Anglo-French issue Vol. 53 (Patricia McCarthy, Ed.)
Manoa: A Pacific Journal of International Writing: Tyranny Lessons (Ming Di,
Alok Bhalla, Frank Stewart, Eds.)
Tab Journal from Chapman University's Tabula Poetica (Anna Leahy,
Ed.)
The Blue Nib (Clara Burghelea, Ed.)
Live Encounters (Mark Ulyseas, Ed.)
The High Window (Timothy Ades, Translation Ed.; David Cook, Ed.)

My deepest gratitude to Diane Seuss, Cynthia Hogue, Martha C⁄
lins, Cyrus Cassells, Lauren Camp, Jason Kampf, Christine Frizz   ,
Christina Zorich, and John FitzGerald for their inspiration and   -
port, and to Dennis Maloney and Elaine LaMattina at Whi   he
Press for delivering this book into the world.

CONTENTS

The Abduction

The Bread of Letters

FOREWORD

Maram Al-Masri's *Le Rapt*, as translated by Hélène Cardona, opens with the simple delights of a mother engaging with her young child, speaking to him as if he is a confidant. "He is occupied / making his ten fingers move / to convince me that love is the natural fruit / of the tree of life," she writes, and what could be more wonderful than that? Bliss, however, is followed by unbearable grief, when her child is abducted and separated from her for years by her then-husband. The poems become the vessel for her dialogue with her missing child, and with her sorrow. Even when mother and child experience a complex reunion years later, each has learned to fear loving the other, and her son must face a second infancy, this time as an immigrant, much less blissful than the first. As a reader of poetry, I am compelled by the raw spareness of these poems, their keen honesty, and their refusal to provide us with a restoration arc. As a parent, I feel empathy, and awe at Al-Masri's survival.

—Diane Seuss,
author of *frank: sonnets*,
winner of the Pulitzer Prize for Poetry
and the National Book Critics Circle Award for Poetry

INTRODUCTION

I discovered Maram Al-Masri when I first read Gabriel Arnou-Laujeac's *Plus loin qu'ailleurs*, for which she wrote the superb French introduction. I fell in love with her lyrical poetry at the same time as with Gabriel Arnou-Laujeac's. In turn, I quoted Maram in my introduction to *Beyond Elsewhere*.

We've since shared numerous phone and email conversations and met in person in Paris to work closely fine-tuning this manuscript. She wrote the original in both Arabic and French and it was important to discuss the nuances. Many of my translations of Maram's poems have been published in literary journals since 2015.

The Abduction refers to an autobiographical event in Al-Masri's life. When, as a young Arab woman living in France, she decides to separate from her husband with whom she has a child, the father kidnaps the baby and returns to Syria. *The Abduction* is the story of a woman who is denied the basic right to raise her child. Al-Masri won't see her son for thirteen years. These are haunting poems of love, despair, and hope in a delicate, profound and powerful book on intimacy, a mother's rights, war, exile, and freedom.

Also included in *The Abduction* is *The Bread of Letters*, comprised of two poems addressing the act of writing: "The act of writing / isn't it a scandalous act in itself? / To write / is learning to know our / most innermost thoughts / Yes I am scandalous / because I show my truth and my nakedness of woman / Yes I am scandalous / because I scream my sorrow and my hope / my desire, my hunger and my thirst."

I excluded the four poems of the short section *Le Semainier* because the French is by another author.

For Al-Masri, writing is a vital and deeply human need: "When I write what I feel, I'm afraid of nothing. Poetry is my freedom and touches me where it lands most deeply. It offers me life vibration, the flush of a river, where feet and dreams meet."

I felt compelled to translate her work to encourage a wider English reading audience to discover her.

While *The Abduction* is the story of a personal tragedy, it also encompasses the global rights of women and children as well as the fate of immigrants and refugees in exile. Al-Masri, exiled in France since 1982, nonetheless reports unflinchingly on the violence and consequences of the unchecked Syrian war.

I was drawn to Al-Masri's work because her stunning, authentic and healing voice is desperately needed in light of the horrendous wars ravaging Syria and the devastating plight of its refugees worldwide. Sandra Jennina writes in *The Daily News*: "For Al-Masri, like many Syrian writers, the recent violence is of an independent nature. It moves from atmospheric to physical; She treats it as a character in her works."

In an article in *Salon*, Maram Al-Masri states, "I'm working in my poetry to tell the truth about my people... What can poetry do in front of all this murder? If the poet doesn't speak, who will do it? Poetry is about freedom; it has always been about freedom... My poems aren't about politics; they are about humans."

In an interview with Deborah Marinacci for *Three Monkeys Online*, Al-Masri declares,

> "I am a free woman... My family sent me to Damascus to study. I used to go to England, and love a boy from a different religion, without hiding. I suffered so much. To them it was somehow insulting, while to me it was moral, honest, non-hypocritical, to me it meant feeling good with the other person, respecting each other. (It meant) to be transparent, harmonize with one's own thoughts."

And in Claire Poinsignon's interview for *Les Nouvelles*, Maram Al-Masri shares that her "poetry shows us the other face of the dead, fallen under the fire of the dictatorship," as well as the face of "international indifference... The other face of people brought to the brink of insanity. The other face of atrocities. Barbarity has no religion. As for me, no one can push me to hate an Alawite (the ethnic and religious group to which Assad belongs). I want to embody the voice of love."

Critic Annalisa Bonomo adds that "what drives Al-Masri's poetic achievements is undoubtedly her truly unique and personal view of the world. Although the author is steeped in her own Syrian cultural background, the real appeal of Al-Masri's verses consists, like any genuine artistic expression, in their capacity to transform a poetic vision into a universally shared experience." Lionel Ray declares that, "behind the simple gestures of daily life, Maram Al-Masri hints at a deep presence. Thus proceeds all true poetry: behind the celebration of the ephemeral, the moment seized by the words resonates with this need in us of the eternal. Like a perfume of Edenic innocence."

For the great Syrian poet Adonis, Maram Al-Masri "expresses all of this in a style that seems to have arisen prior to art, as if it were purely formless or a project, as if writing was an organic, non-technical issue. She expresses this passion in everyday language, simple, warm, irrepressible, on the verge of meeting her body, but stopping almost at the edge of language."

And André Ughetto calls her poems "the 'diary' of a quest for love, as well as of its disenchantment. Her "song" reveals her concerns, including that of remaining in exile in her own poetic language: "Her children inherit... A mother who writes poems / in a language they don't understand."

As a translator, I see myself as intermediary, technician, and alchemist working between languages to create inspired texts spanning cultural differences, geographic distances, and time. I strive to capture the essence of the poem while remaining as close as possible to it, knowing that I'm creating a new piece at the same time. My goal is to transcend the original and give it its own voice in English.

Translation is also une histoire d'amour. When you understand and know other cultures, you don't fear the other. There is no other. Every language is a key into the psyche of its people. None of us would understand our roots without translation.

I couldn't agree more with Anne Michaels when she writes, "Translation is a kind of transubstantiation; one poem becomes another." Translation is a craft. It is also an inspired act, a negotiation. To quote Henry James, "We work in the dark," from that intuitive place. It becomes an act of revelation, the ultimate act of sympathy." Anton Chekhov wrote in a letter that translation is the art of existing in two languages at once. Language, thinking and writing are connected. When you're in a different land, surrounded by a different language, you think differently.

Poetry redeems, heals, changes lives. It has the power to bring us together by unifying experience. It is both personal and universal. It enriches and contributes to the fullness of human life. Maram Al-Masri's poetry finds echoes in Marguerite Duras' words: "Writing comes like the wind. It's naked, it's made of ink, it's the thing written, and it passes like nothing else passes in life, nothing more, except life itself." It leaves us astonished.

—Hélène Cardona

Your children are not yours. They are the children of life.
And life does not reside in yesterday's house.

—Kahlil Gibran

THE ABDUCTION

Nine months

Nine months
and life grows in the womb
like a poem grows in imagination
Nine months
and a body grows inside another body
Nine months
and the wait weaves hope and dreams
Nine months
for silence to grow
into a cry
like a loaf of bread rising
or round moon
reaching fullness
Nine months
for a heart to flutter
inside a heart
Nine months
for a life to begin

We sow

We sow
she sprouts
she grows
she hurts
she explodes
she gives birth
to an infant in a poem

Between her thighs
he flows
like a waterfall
a small body
naked
warm
He cries,
I am here

He has begun to speak to me

He has begun to speak to me
with his eight tiny teeth
drool on his lips
he tells me
with his eyes
things that seem to him very important
perhaps he is telling me about the war
and the children born
to die every day
or perhaps
he speaks
of faraway islands, of birds
of dreams
of crises
of famines

I don't know if he wants to tell me
the future will be sunny
and a day will come
when people live in peace

He is occupied
making his ten fingers move
to convince me that love is the natural fruit
of the tree of life
and that he is happy
to have come into this world

Then, suddenly, he embraces me
burrowing his head into my chest
begging me to take him in my arms
In that instant I understand
all that he wants to tell me

I hugged him

I hugged him
I felt his peaceful breathing
moisten my neck

I cuddled him on my breast
I caressed his face
I touched with my fingers
the innocence of his skin
an instant of eternity bloomed
into a desert day

I still feel his hands
on my shoulders
and on my chin
the pain from his tiny teeth

Like a duck

Like a duck
you waddle
and take three steps
you cling to my finger
If I release you, you fall again
I pick you up and hum
you walk haltingly
like a duck
you fall and get back up
we try again
we fall, get up
Such is
life
my little rascal
'til we become horses
galloping

Caught in the act

Caught in the act
busy disorganizing
the contents of drawers
and throwing whatever his hands
can reach all over
he runs away
hiding his face, then slowly, gently turns
to observe my reaction
and when he sees a smile
on my lips
he comes back, arms outstretched, implores
and invokes my weakness
then climbs upon me
as if nothing ever happened

Come on, sun

Come on, sun
wake up!
Let your yellow hair float
over the shivering shoulders of the earth,
over the houses and the streets.
Heat up stones and asphalt—
dance, sun, ablaze!
Make this day a beautiful day,
because far from this cold wall
in a field of colors
where the sky is made of tales
and where the trees are poems
I will take my little one for a walk.

In such beautiful weather

In such beautiful weather
I need my little one
so I can rejoice with him
in the sky, the water,
the people.

In weather sad as this
I need my little one
so I can rejoice
and make him rejoice
in life.

Dance, dance

Dance, dance
my son
for you were born
to teach the birds
to fly

dance, dance
my son
that the restless heart of the world
may calm itself
to the rhythm of your steps

dance, dance
my son
that you may learn to fly

I talk to him

I talk to him
as to a friend
converse with him
as one would with grown ups
I ask him if he likes my red dress
its length
Would it be better longer?
After putting on my makeup, I ask him
how he finds me
Am I beautiful?
Primping his belly
and his cheeks
with my red lips
overjoys me
while he is busy emptying
the drawer of its spoons

With these two hands

With these two hands
I prepare your suitcase
your father tells me
he's going to take you on a short trip
to a city by the sea

in your suitcase I pack
your finest clothes
for my little one goes for a walk by the sea

I also pack
cakes you love
a water bottle
and everything you might need
for my little one goes for a walk by the sea

with these two hands
I place you in your stroller
happy
for my little one goes for a walk by the sea

the first night passed
and to this day
my little one's stroller has not returned

O human brothers

O human brothers
O world
I had a child
I hid him in my belly
He shared my body
I nourished him with my blood
I shared my dreams with him
I sang for him, he smiled
I carried him, he stopped crying

He was torn from my arms
I stopped singing

War rages in Rwanda

War rages in Rwanda
and me, I eat
War rages in Yugoslavia
and me, I smile
War rages in Palestine
and me, I sleep

but since you were kidnapped
war rages within me

In the evening

In the evening
when my flowers have faded
I curl up under a heavy blanket
I close my eyes
and wonder:
what dreams
can sleep
deign to bring me?

Promise me

Promise me
if I close my eyes
you will run into my arms
and brighten
this dark world

Promise me
if I open my eyes
you will stay

I sent you

I sent you
my love
by mail
I fashioned it into small toys
so you could play
I fashioned it into a woolen polo shirt
so you'd be warm.

I sent you my love
by mail
I traded it for two boxes of aspirin
a toothbrush
cakes, chocolates
a bicycle
Did you receive the package?

If I smile while you're away

If I smile while you're away
it means a shadow
has passed in front of me
you in white layers
and the toy you drag behind

if I smile while you're away
it doesn't mean I've forgotten you
but sometimes
it means
your presence
even thousands of miles away
can bring me happiness

Forgive me, my little one

Forgive me, my little one
if I couldn't come quickly
on foot, the path is long
and tickets dear

forgive me, my little one
this excuse
must seem feeble to you
surely
I could come on foot
borrow the money
or save some
quit smoking
(though I don't smoke)
even sell my mother's jewels
to pay for tickets

forgive them, my little one
when I arrived
they would not let me see you

Far from my arms

Far from my arms
you sleep in a bed that isn't yours
you no longer see my face
nor my eyes looking at you with such love
you can no longer take my hands
the way you used to
before falling asleep

At night you'll wake
and say *Mama*
to a woman who is not me

Far from my eyes
you will grow up
go to school
and I will not be waiting for you at the gate
When you're sick
I won't be worrying by your side

I won't know your face or voice
I won't know your smell
or the size of your shoes
You'll remain in my memory
an eighteen-month-old child
kidnapped from me

I came back home

I came back home
after a night out with friends
in a hurry to be with you again

I cracked open the door
pricking up my ears
in the silence to measure
how deeply you slept

tonight
I came into your room
the bed was quiet
covered with your soul
and yet I swear
I heard you breathing

Every morning

Every morning
I wake
hoping to prepare your meal

every morning
I open my eyes
wishing you could wet
my face with kisses

every morning I wake
wishing you'd woken me
much earlier
having fragmented my sleep
to smithereens

Remember

Remember
that little boy
who lived with his parents near us?
Remember
when his mom would leave him with us
while she went shopping?
I'd bring you together
to play and babble

Remember
how quiet and well-behaved he was?
He wouldn't complain
or get annoyed when you took his toys
or leaned on him to stand

His name was Salim
his mother, Josephine, a resigned woman
had tasted bitterness, like me
When I learned that his father
had kidnapped him
and sent him away to his grandmother's
I wept for Salim
In that moment I didn't know
I was shedding my first tears
for you

Under the bed

Under the bed
I found the teddy bear
you smothered with kisses
the one you talked to, eyes wide open
waiting for the angel of sleep to come

Remember how it stopped
the storm of your cries
when I waved it at you
'til the night of your eyes glistened
and even the Niagara Falls
stopped falling

You tore it from my hands
clutching it against you
soothed
It was your companion
to face the night
your silent friend
the one you neglected when busy
the one you looked for when sad

The teddy bear and angel of sleep
keep looking for you

I'm not so old

I'm not so old
so why
do I feel this way?
Why has the hair of my dreams turned white?
why has the shine of my eyes
turned to ash?

I'm not so old
so why
can I no longer taste the honey of life?
And why has the morning song
I used to hum
become silent?

I don't want to grow old

I don't want to grow old
so my child recognizes me
the day he comes back
to see me

I don't want to die
like my mother
because I have a child
though not in my arms
but one day
for certain
he will need me

I promise you, Mother

I promise you, Mother
all is well

Let your body rest as much as possible
sleep gently
and don't let nightmares disturb your peace

Tonight, you needn't
free your soul
to roam about the house

Your little children have grown
the eldest boy married just after you left us
you know his wife, who was my friend
Now they have two children
He gave the first-born his father's name

You can be proud of the second,
whose absence made you weep with worry
because he married too
You don't know his wife
but you would love her
He has a child to whom he gave his father's name

As for the third, so spoiled,
it's true he doesn't work but don't worry
one day he will
and don't be surprised if one day he gets married
perhaps he'll give his first-born
his father's name

I don't know if you know
that my sister and I
both also married

Me, I'm divorced
Don't panic
it's not so bad
except if you'd been there
my child wouldn't have been taken from me
But no need to be sad
as you are far from pain and time
I saw your friend yesterday
my God, how she's changed!
She's grown old and is losing her teeth
You, young woman
you will remain like the day you closed your eyes
You may have done well
so you won't see
even if I tell you otherwise
that my father remarried
and that we are truly orphans without you

I no longer have the patience

I no longer have the patience
to do the housework
I no longer have the energy
to take out the trash
I no longer have the spirit
to put up with jokes
that don't make me laugh
I no longer have the strength to give birth
to wishes that color the day
nor have I a breast that gives milk

So I swing my arms
and there is no child in my lap
I look out a window
I haven't cleaned for a long time
The world is cold

From my window

From my window
I see houses
their windows often closed
I imagine what moves
behind those thick walls
I see a man returning home
and a woman going out
wearing a black coat
They have two children
life has allowed them to watch grow

A house like mine
may be hiding wounds
may be hiding stories

One Sunday
the day of the feast of love
I see the man coming back
to his house
with a bouquet of flowers
A house that is not mine
dresses in joy

I wait for you when I'm awake

I wait for you when I'm awake
I wait for you when I'm asleep
I wait for you when I smile
I wait for you when I weep
I wait for you when I breathe
I wait for you
when I'm not waiting for you
I wait for you like a page in a book
like a long-lasting hunger
I wait for you
like a breast full of milk
I wait for you like a seashore
I wait for you like a festive garment
I wait for you like an unread letter
I wait for you like hope
I wait for you like a hot meal
I wait for you like dawn
I wait for you
like a mother

Dusk no longer has your eyes

Dusk no longer has your eyes
resting between your eyelids
Dusk no longer has a home
It saunters
in its black robe into my heart

Asleep on my shoulder, dusk
resembles your hair
I would like to nestle there
and inhale your scent
and wake in the morning
damp from your kisses

My dusk no longer has trees
sway in its shadow
since you've been gone

Blessed are those who sleep deeply

Blessed are those who sleep deeply
me, I sleep like the guardians of the world
eyes half-closed
like a mother lying with a newborn
in her arms, suckling her milk
her ears attentive to his breathing

First encounter

First encounter

How you've grown my son!
you've grown for thirteen years
and your mouth
is full of teeth
the clothes I kept for you no longer fit
neither do the shoes

Do you think
we'd have recognized each other
had we met by chance?

Look at me

Look at me
do you remember me .
I'm the one who brought you into the world
who gave you milk

Look at your brothers
I've told you so much about them
say hello to them in French
it's enough
to kiss them
or exchange a smile

They don't resemble you
you are more brown
but if we look closely
we see you share
the same traits

Let's go
repeat their names after me
Mathieu, yes Mathieu
Guill ... aume
you see it's not so difficult
to speak
the language of love

Five years after our encounter

Five years after our encounter
I walked away from the noise
he followed me
sat near me
I dared put my head on his shoulder
I wanted to breathe his air
and recover the faded smell of his infancy

I took his hands in mine
they were moist and sticky
he started to count my fingers
for him I had a thousand

in the disquieting silence
save for the chatter of his heart
and breath
he asked in a trembling voice
are you afraid to love me?

how can a woman like me
be afraid to love
when within her live
all paths
all songs
all kisses
all smiles?
I answered
yes

he nodded
smiling
so the words fell all around us
like the feathers of a wounded bird

he answered
me too

To confront so much pain

To confront so much pain
and shatter the statue of sorrow
I sprinkle my smile
like flower pollen
on the treetops
electricity pylons
sidewalks
the faces of passers-by
bread
my cup of coffee

to be worthy of love
I sow love

Each morning

Each morning
I cover myself in a dew of tears
each day I cry
in the streets
in the subway
at the movie theater
in bed
in dreams
in tenderness
but
I deliver my smiles
like a postman

Each day I kill myself a little
to stay alive

At my door, two suitcases

At my door, two suitcases
and a young man
tall and slim
dark brown
hesitant like one who has lost his way

At my door, two worn suitcases
like dock workers' clothes
in the port of a poor city

they carry the scent of distant lands
memories
histories
like a prisoner's chains

a young, dark brown man
with black hair
his black eyes
aswim in a white sea

he knocks on the door
of my heart

The world is hard, my son

The world is hard, my son
hard as a machine gun magazine
hard as the walls of a detention center
hard as the look of contempt
I didn't warn you to wait before coming to join me
I didn't warn you, little plants
get easily trampled
I didn't warn you, here you must be strong
here they like diplomas
they like bank accounts
I warn you, the drowned
cannot save
the drowning

Immigrant
you will always be
in the crosshairs of suspicion
I didn't warn you, immigrants arrive fragile
as infants

To love

To love
is to give another
the possibility of doing without you
To love, it is to prepare yourself
to be abandoned

Why do we love them?

Why do we love them?
we love them because we've seen them
as small bundles of cotton in our hands
we sometimes see them as rare objects
then at times we see them
and hope they become distinct
like movie actors
like photocopies of our dreams
and yet we love them

we love them even when they grow ugly
become obese
hide behind their beards
turn dark and violent like a slap
we love them with their smelly socks
their acne
their illnesses
their failures

we love them mentally impaired
disabled
we love them even when they're wrong
take drugs
lose their way
and even
irredeemable

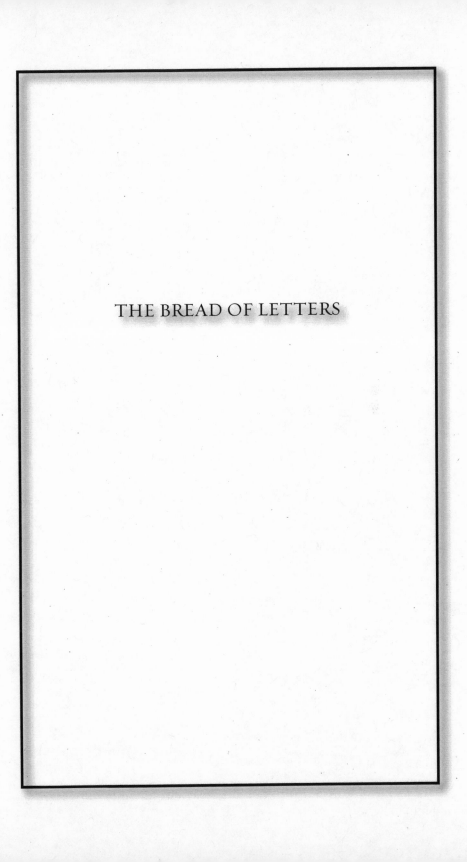

THE BREAD OF LETTERS

The Bread of Letters

I

Who will blame the trees
when they loose their leaves?
who will accuse the sea of abandoning shells on the sand?

I, mother-woman, woman-mother
with two breasts for pleasure
and two breasts for maternity
who give the milk of music
tell stories
explain games
light up feelings
and the grammar of thoughts
I, woman of delight
and tenderness
virtuous and sinful
mature and childlike
with my mouth
I feed the bread of letters
consonants and vowels
sentences, synonyms and comparisons.

Who will accuse me
of making a gift of my body
to love?

II

The act of writing
isn't it a scandalous act in itself?

To write
is learning to know our most intimate thoughts

Yes I am scandalous
because I show my truth and my nakedness of woman

Yes I am scandalous
because I scream my sorrow and my hope
my desire, my hunger and my thirst

To write
is to describe the multiple faces of man
the beautiful and the ugly
the tender and the cruel

To write is to die in front of someone
who looks at you, unmoved

it is to drown in front of a boat passing you by
without seeing you

To write
is to be the boat that saves the drowning

To write
is to live on the cliff's edge
clinging to a blade
of grass

When I write, my self belongs to the other
With this conviction
I am freed.

The Author

Maram Al-Masri was born in Latakia, Syria, and moved to France following the completion of English Literature studies at Damascus University. Her books include *Métropoèmes, Je te regarde, Cerise rouge sur un carrelage blanc, Le Rapt, Elle va nue la liberté, Par la fontaine de ma bouche* (Bruno Doucey), *A Red Cherry on a White-tiled Floor* (Copper Canyon), and the anthology *Femmes poètes du monde arabe*.

Al-Masri's literary prizes include the Prix d'Automne 2007 de Poésie de la Société des Gens De Lettres, the Adonis Prize, the Premio Citta di Calopezzati, Il Fiore d'Argento, and the Dante Alighieri Prize.

She is a member of the Parlement des écrivaines francophones and was appointed Ambassador of the Secours Populaire in France and citoyenne d'honneur of Vendenheim. In 2017, the Maram Al-Masri Prize was created, which rewards poetry and graphic works.

Photo ©Philippe Barnoud

The Translator

Hélène Cardona's books include *Life in Suspension* and *Dreaming My Animal Selves* (both Salmon Poetry) and the translations *Birnam Wood* (José Manuel Cardona, Salmon Poetry), *Beyond Elsewhere* (Gabriel Arnou-Laujeac, White Pine Press), *Ce que nous portons* (Dorianne Laux, Éditions du Cygne), and *Walt Whitman's Civil War Writings* (University of Iowa's WhitmanWeb).

She has also translated André Breton, Rimbaud, Baudelaire, Aloysius Bertrand, Eric Sarner, René Depestre, Ernest Pépin, Jean-Claude Renard, Nicolas Grenier, Christiane Singer, Lea Nagy, and John Ashbery. Her own work has been translated into seventeen languages.

The recipient of over twenty honors and awards, including the Independent Press Award and a Hemingway Grant, she holds an MA in American Literature from the Sorbonne, received fellowships from the Goethe-Institut and Universidad Internacional de Andalucía, worked as a translator for the Canadian Embassy, and taught at Hamilton College and Loyola Marymount University. She is a member of the Parlement des écrivaines francophones.